Meet the Bearded Dragon

Suzanne Buckingham

PowerKiDS press.
New York

To the Nader family, Gregg, Patty, Robby, Andy, Lily, and their bearded dragon, Spikey

Published in 2009 by The Rosen Publishing Group, Inc.
29 East 21st Street, New York, NY 10010

First Edition

Editor: Joanne Randolph
Book Design: Greg Tucker
Photo Researcher: Jessica Gerweck

Photo Credits: Back cover, cover (logo), cover photo, pp. 5, 6, 12–13, 14, 17, 21 Shutterstock.com; p. 9 © Matt Meadows/Peter Arnold, Inc.; p. 10 © Stefan Mokrzecki/Superstock; p. 18 © Steimer, C./Peter Arnold, Inc.

Library of Congress Cataloging-in-Publication Data

Buckingham, Suzanne.
  Meet the bearded dragon / Suzanne Buckingham. — 1st ed.
      p. cm. — (Scales and tails)
  Includes index.
  ISBN 978-1-4042-4500-6 (library binding)
  1. Bearded dragons (Reptiles)—Juvenile literature. I. Title.
  QL666.L223B83 2009
  597.95'5—dc22
                              2008003480

Manufactured in the United States of America

Contents

Meet the Bearded Dragon

Some people may think bearded dragons are scary. Perhaps that is because they have bumpy **scales** all over their bodies, sharp **spikes**, and large mouths. You do not need to be afraid of these gentle animals, though. Many people keep bearded dragons as pets.

A bearded dragon's tiny scales and pointed spikes help keep it safe. Its hard scales form a shell that guards it from enemies. Bearded dragons are interesting lizards that are full of surprises. Did you know that most will "wave" to visitors by moving one front leg in a circle? Let's find out more about these friendly lizards called beardies.

Here you can see the scales all over the bearded dragon's body. You can also see the points under its chin that give the lizard its name.

This bearded dragon has puffed out its beard and opened its mouth. It is trying to scare an enemy away.

What About the Beard?

The bearded dragon got its name from the pouch of skin under its chin that looks like a beard. When a beardie sees an enemy, it will puff out this pouch to scare the enemy away. When the lizard is in danger, this skin also turns dark purple or black. Some bearded dragons open their mouths to appear scarier.

All beardies, both **male** and **female**, have beards. The beards are also used when these lizards **mate**. The male will puff out his beard and bob his head up and down to try to get a female's attention.

Kinds of Bearded Dragons

There are eight kinds of bearded dragons. Each one lives in a different part of Australia.

The dwarf bearded dragon is found in the middle and western parts of this warm place. This small lizard has short legs and a short tail. The inland bearded dragon is larger than the dwarf. It lives in the dry, central part of Australia. Inland beardies are yellow to brown in color. Their exact shade depends on the soil color. The eastern bearded dragon is darker than the inland beardie and has larger spikes. It stays on Australia's eastern and southern coasts.

This is an eastern bearded dragon. This beardie likes to sit in trees but also spends time on the ground.

This bearded dragon makes its home in the desert of Australia's Northern Territory. It sits in the sun to warm itself.

Beardie Homes

Bearded dragons live in many different **habitats** found in Australia, such as deserts, forests, caves, and wet places near the coast. Beardies are **cold-blooded** animals. Their bodies cannot make heat, so they must sit in the sunlight to stay warm. Bearded dragons **bask** in the bright sun for hours on top of logs, rocks, and fences.

If these creatures get too hot, they move into the shade or underground **burrows**. At night, bearded dragons may crawl into burrows to stay warm.

The Bearded Dragon

Male bearded dragons have larger heads and darker beards than females.

Bearded dragons may let out a loud hiss to scare enemies away when they puff out their beards.

Scaly Facts

- A bearded dragon's tail is almost as long as its body.
- Bearded dragons are semiarboreal, which means they spend some of their time living in trees.
- Inland bearded dragons live 4 to 10 years.
- The small-scaled bearded dragon lives in the woodlands of the northwestern part of Australia. This lizard has fewer spikes on its back and throat than most beardies.
- A ripe banana usually draws fruit flies, which make a tasty snack for bearded dragons.
- Beardies enjoy eating all kinds of bugs, but snacking on just one firefly can kill a bearded dragon.
- The length of an adult inland bearded dragon is between 18 and 22 inches (46–56 cm).
- Adults shed their outer layer of skin several times a year.

This bearded dragon has caught a grasshopper. Bugs like this give the beardie important nutrients.

Dinner with a Bearded Dragon

If you have a bearded dragon over for dinner, you can serve it almost anything! These animals are not picky eaters. Bearded dragons are omnivorous, which means they eat both plants and animals.

Beardies living in the wild eat many plant parts, such as fruits, leaves, and flowers. They also enjoy munching on different kinds of bugs. Large bearded dragons may dine on small animals, such as mice and other lizards. Beardies can eat a lot at one meal because they have very large stomachs.

Watch Out, Beardies!

To stay safe from enemies, beardies must be careful. For example, the tiny Lawson's bearded dragon is a favorite meal for many large snakes. If this beardie sees a snake coming near, it looks for a large crack in the dirt in which to hide. A large lizard called a monitor is another enemy. The monitor uses its long, forked **tongue** to smell where tasty beardies are hiding.

Some bearded dragons face human-made dangers. Western bearded dragons often bask on roads in Western Australia. Drivers do not always see these sunning beardies in time!

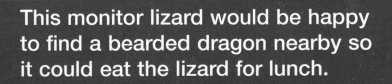

This monitor lizard would be happy to find a bearded dragon nearby so it could eat the lizard for lunch.

Here you can see a clutch of eggs in a burrow. The mother beardie sits on top of the burrow.

The Life of a Bearded Dragon

After mating, a female bearded dragon digs a burrow for her eggs. An inland bearded dragon lays a group of up to 24 eggs. This group of eggs is called a clutch. A mother beardie covers her clutch with dirt to keep it safe.

After about 65 days, tiny inland bearded dragons **hatch** from their eggs. The new babies are hungry. They quickly start looking for food to eat. Bearded dragons become adults when they are about one to two years old. Soon, these adults lay eggs of their own, and the **cycle** begins again.

Baby Beardies

After hatching, a new beardie does not have parents nearby to watch over it. This small, helpless lizard must hide from enemies under plants and rocks. It also searches for small insects to eat.

An inland bearded dragon is a little more than 3 inches (8 cm) long when it is born. It grows to twice that length by the time it is two months old. At five months, it will measure 10 inches (25 cm) long. The bearded dragon will reach its adult length by one year. Baby beardies quickly grow into long, strong lizards!

This is a young
bearded dragon.
As pets, some
bearded dragons
are known to live
10 to 15 years.

21

Bearded Dragons and People

The inland bearded dragon is one of the most popular pet **reptiles** in the United States. These animals are very social. They often bob their heads when they see other bearded dragons or people. Beardies also love to be held.

To keep pet beardies healthy, owners must take them to the vet for checkups. Beardies also need lots of good food. Bearded dragons like fruits and vegetables such as lettuce, berries, and green carrot tops. They also enjoy crunchy crickets and juicy mealworms. Bearded dragons are friendly pets that enjoy the company of people.

Glossary

bask (BASK) To lie in the sun.

burrows (BUR-ohz) Holes animals dig in the ground to live in.

cold-blooded (KOHLD-bluh-did) Having a body heat that changes with the heat around the body.

cycle (SY-kul) Actions that happen in the same order over and over.

female (FEE-mayl) Having to do with women and girls.

habitats (HA-beh-tats) The kinds of land where animals or plants naturally live.

hatch (HACH) To come out of an egg.

male (MAYL) Having to do with men or boys.

mate (MAYT) To join together to make babies.

reptiles (REP-tylz) Cold-blooded animals with scales.

scales (SKAYLZ) Thin, dry pieces of skin that form the outer covering of snakes, lizards, and other reptiles.

spikes (SPYKS) Sharp, pointy things shaped like spears or needles.

tongue (TUNG) A part inside the mouths of animals that helps the animals take in and swallow food.

Index

Web Sites

Due to the changing nature of Internet links, PowerKids Press has developed an online list of Web sites related to the subject of this book. This site is updated regularly. Please use this link to access the list:
www.powerkidslinks.com/scat/bdrag/